TEEN LOVE

TEEN LOVE

SLOANE MONTGOMERY

CONTENTS

CHAPTER 1

Introduction to Teen Love

Children, from a young age, are continually inundated with ideas about relationships and love. As they mature into adolescence, these relationships and infatuations become less about crushes and more about finding real, long-lasting emotional connections with others. During this period, teenagers begin dating. How parents and other adults respond to teen love often involves one of two ends of the spectrum: some may deny that it exists, while others may become overprotective, minimizing their child's emotions. In actuality, teenagers' feelings about relationships can be all-consuming and help them develop into more mature, emotionally intelligent adults.

Certainly, adults recognize that infatuations and dating among teenagers are not the same as when they grow older and relationships are likely to last longer and become more serious. But discussions about teen love as an aspect of adolescence — like self-identity, emotions, and relationships — are just as important for families, teachers, and other adults who interact with teenagers every day. Understanding what goes through the minds of teenagers as they grapple with relationships, crushes, and sometimes heartbreak can help adults provide a more stable and supportive environment. It is common for everybody to feel sad every now and then, and every emotion has its place. Understanding the myriad of emotions teens feel in relationships is an important step toward recognizing that "life lessons" about love and relationships begin from a very young age.

Defining Teen Love

Teen love, we believe, has unique characteristics that, when cultivated, can bring many positives to teens' lives. When we talk about "love" in "teen love," we are trying to capture many different levels of tenderness, care, affection, sexual attraction, and interest in each other. While teenage love can be quite passionate and physically intimate, many times "love" refers to emotional and cognitive closeness rather than physical or sexual behavior per se. However, being in love, especially with a "crush" or boyfriend or girlfriend, often means that teens have feelings of erotic attraction (teenaged "lust"), positive emotional emotions (such as "desire," "attraction," and "affection"), and a wish to be with or to hug and kiss the person they're in "love" with.

From a developmental perspective, research finds that romantic partners play a special role in teens' emotional lives. Peers drive one another to develop a sense of self and to get to know oneself in response to another person who matters. Romantic partners play an important role in this broader peer story. Partners actively teach one another about themselves and themselves in relation to others, and these experiences aid in identity development. Teen love is a potentially life-altering experience shaping the development of how teens think about themselves and pursue future close relationships as well as impacting their current family relationships.

CHAPTER 2

Understanding Adolescence and Emotions

The decade-and-a-half between childhood and adulthood can be a difficult one for emotional reasons. A teenager's cognitive and emotional development is in a blender that fluctuates day to day or even moment to moment. Understanding how and why the teen you know keeps breaking up and getting back together or crying over a crush or not taking anything seriously requires a broader look at where they are and why.

The teen years bring about the same developmental changes in the brain as the "terrible twos," but with a few extra layers of turmoil. Spatial reasoning, memory, and information management have a good head start by the time puberty hits, so most teens are not as impaired in those areas as a two-year-old might be. Morality, decision making, impulses, and other cognitive and emotional changes will all flood the system through till 25 or beyond. Knowing about this process can help adults through the spot where most adults pull out their sighs – dead-end teen relationships: how teens navigate crushes and that first inkling of love.

Young people are acting out love dynamics while they're learning to cope with emotions as deep and dark as orphanhood or failure. This is different from adults and kids as young as 4 or 6 playing "house" or "doctor." It requires an understanding of what goes into a relationship, what is fun and flirty, and what are challenging and/or harmful dynamics. It informs the ability to see what could be an empathetic joke from a friend versus a belittling barb from an antagonizer. We treat teens' heartache as a sort of natural, remediable rite of passage. There can be denial because it seems so insignificant on the scale of Other Possible Teen Drama. But for the fledgling teen heart, which is asking questions like "am I lovable?" "does anyone really know me?" "can I trust anybody?" "does anybody have my back?" – this is anything but mild.

Developmental Psychology in Adolescence

Adolescence is a distinct period of development. It is sandwiched between the newfound independence of preschoolhood and the budding autonomy of adulthood. Physiologically, it entails hormonal changes that rapidly alter a child's physical features and increase sexual and reproductive function. These changes affect each boy and girl differently, sometimes leading to an exaggerated shift in mood and increased worry. Unfortunately, dramatic shifts in the brain also occur during adolescence and interfere with a child's ability to think clearly, manage emotions well, and exhibit self-control. Researchers continue to study structural and functional changes in the brain that lead to or are precipitated by cognitive lag and may subsequently impact a teenager's ability to engage in effective decision making. Understanding these changes is particularly useful because they can provide context for the reasons some teenagers engage in risky behaviors including early sexual onset and partnering with older, more experienced peers.

Cognitive development also undergoes rapid change. Strong evidence suggests that latent intellectual abilities are enriched over time; regardless, the rapidity and apparent comfort with which they develop change dramatically as he or she enters school and even further upon entering puberty. Preadolescence, in particular, is a period during which children's physical, emotional, and social conflict may appear off-balance with their developing adolescent-sized mental capacities. Emotional and empathic shifts take place during adolescence in conjunction with increased self-awareness. Not only extraordinary physical changes, but also the intensity of emotional reactions characterizes the adolescent stage of development. A myriad of social, emotional, and hormonal changes influence teenagers' craving to engage in love relationships and sex coupled with a notable immaturity in judging potential consequences of intimate contact.

CHAPTER 3

Building Healthy Relationships

Feeling puny in the face of X's glowing charm and shiny new Jeep? No swag in being beside Y when you're pining for Z? Our society really puts pressure on people to be part of a couple. You don't have to be. Being with someone who doesn't respect your true feelings is a lonely business. True companionship is about communicating and sharing your personal beliefs. Involvement with someone who hears your thoughts builds self-confidence. To have a healthy relationship with others, you need three C's. Communication: it's better to not blame or criticize others; the problem is with how you feel about things. Clarification: it's more important to have a positive perspective than to be "right". Remember, goals are how you both want to behave. No one likes someone who's right all the time. Collaboration: it's alright to express anger once in a while. Let the other person know how you feel.

Nurturing Relationships: In healthy relationships, you support each other's goals and learn about each other's needs and feelings. Healthy couples value each other's opinions, talk openly, and honor their promise to stand by each other. Relationships don't cover up our problems or make us happy. We all come with our own problems; we all have our own emotions. We need to recognize our feelings before we can work through them positively. All relationships have their ups and downs. Ups bring us happiness and pleasure; downs can make us sick, anxious, or depressed. The skills needed for a healthy relationship can be learned at any time. With practice, we can learn to avoid conflict and tolerate differences. If we are able to identify our own feelings, we can not only understand others' feelings but appreciate them.

Communication Skills in Relationships

Existing research indicates the importance of open and honest communication in fostering a close and emotionally intimate bond between romantic partners. The ability to express feelings and concerns is an essential component of a healthy, working relationship. People have different communication styles, but when both partners are comfortable expressing themselves through words and actions, it can keep a relationship healthy and connected. For teens, this skillset may lead to maintaining their relationship, breaking up in a more respectful way, or learning how to manage heartache in a healthy way.

Learn to Speak in "I Feel" Statements: Teenage "love" relationships can be quite tense and passionate. A great way to avoid a shouting match over something is to ensure that they know a strategy to effectively diffuse a tense conversation. This often means they need to be able to simply and accurately describe their emotions and the reasons why they are angry or hurt. If they can do this without the argument spiraling out of their control, it is less likely to make their partner angry with them. They also become less likely to be misunderstood.

Practice Empathy and Understanding: Unity is a wonderful thing. It makes people feel connected and avoids a lot of heartaches. In the process of an argument, they should "view" the other person's view as their own view. This also helps prevent taking things personally. Teens should also talk to them in a warm voice and make sure to say that they understand where they are coming from.

CHAPTER 4

Navigating Crushes and Infatuation

Why can't I stop thinking about my crush? Part of being a teen means navigating infatuation, crushes, romantic feelings, and heartbreak. These details for the teen dating section can help you better understand and support your child as they explore this new world of feelings. It is normal for kids of all ages to have a crush on someone and for these feelings to be painful sometimes. It is good to let your child know that having a crush and feeling sad or embarrassed when things don't work out is normal. Even if they only like someone because they are in the same class or because they are good at a sport, your child still feels the way they do.

When kids have a "crush" on someone, the feeling is usually more about wanting to be around someone rather than really loving the person. A giddy feeling is common. Usually, kids who have a crush on someone feel lighthearted, but sometimes having a crush can feel like extreme emotions of anger and sadness. It is rare, however, for kids younger than 9 years of age to have intense feelings of attraction. Having a crush on someone is part of being a teenager. You've probably experienced a "crush" on someone. You've recently had romantic feelings towards someone if you are a teenager. If this is true, you may have many unanswered questions about attraction, crushes, and love within a framework of Christian beliefs. A crush refers to feelings of infatuation or attraction towards someone that are usually temporary and non-romantic. An infatuation is a very strong crush. When you develop a "crush" on someone, you think about the person a lot. It doesn't necessarily mean that you "like like" (romantically like) the person.

Differentiating Between Crushes and Love

There's a reason why this book is written for teenagers, specifically, and not for anyone else. It's because it provides information and help with issues that affect people who are somewhere between the ages of, say, 12 to 18 called "the teen years." There are other books about love too. Some of them were written for adults, some for college students, and some were written for teenagers your age. Throughout time, poets, storytellers, songwriters, and moviemakers have described what it feels like to start feeling "love." But, as we're sure you've noticed, not all of these descriptions of love are the same because not everyone feels the same kind of love or the same way about it when they're your age.

In this book, we want to help you figure out if your feelings about love are similar to infatuation, a crush, being in love, or something else. As suggested in the opening story of this "Crushing, Dating, and Breaking Up" chapter, feeling "love" for someone or having a "crush" can make a big difference in what your days are like. From when you get up to when you go to sleep, your thoughts, feelings, and actions can be affected by the people you are privately growing fond of or causing you to fall deeply in love with someone. Endless thoughts about this special someone may not leave you alone - even the thought of that person might not leave you alone. It might feel like your whole life revolves around your feelings and reactions toward someone else. You might even notice that feelings of love might turn you into someone different than usual. Do you notice that sometimes there's something about you or the way you come across to your friends, family, or other people that's not quite the same as it was before? It can be hard to know what's going on when you have strong feelings.

CHAPTER 5

Dealing with Heartbreak and Rejection

Dealing with heartbreak is never easy. If you've recently been through a break-up or been rejected by your crush, it's likely you're not feeling your best. But, along with the negative emotions you're feeling, heartbreak can also be a time of personal growth. Dealing with rejection and heartbreak can help you learn new coping mechanisms and to be more open and resilient. In addition, if you still have feelings for your ex or your crush, getting over the heartache can make you emotionally available to meet someone who can love and appreciate you the way you deserve.

Teenage relationships can be intense and almost all teens will experience the pain of unrequited love at some point or another. A massive study found that the average age for getting over a break-up was about three months but there are many additional factors such as prior heartache, a difficult break-up, a long-loved ex, and sharing friends or identity with your ex, to name a few. What's more, not all relationships last, so if you get dumped a couple of weeks after entering a relationship, you're likely to feel a little differently than if you were broken up with after you'd been together for years – and that's okay. Not every person will deal with a break-up in the same way at the same time.

Coping Mechanisms for Heartbreak

It is okay to feel awful after being rejected or after a first heartbreak, whether it is over a breakup or just unrequited puppy love. It is okay to feel the emotion fully and not to turn everything off. It's okay not to want to take a nap or anything else right away, no matter how much time has passed. It is okay to take a nap or just sit around feeling sad for a little while before taking the next step. However, if they take too long feeling sad—the kinds of situations that should be their tell-tale sign they should reach out to someone else to chat—then they should seek help. It is okay to instill some hope in new relationships.

In the dark, after a rejection, tell oneself one good thing about him or herself. It is not such a small thing, really. Rejection is personal. It is a reflection of the value he or she has that the other person does not see. It would be surprising if no one in the world could knock someone off guard, even if ever so slightly. Besides, heartbreak either directly or indirectly can stir up so many different negative emotions and cause forgetfulness. Therefore, establishing some "defensive" means of reconstructing the reality is a good step forward. With those things in mind and because they have a reverberatory effect within a person, with enough practice and time, there is a fair chance that they will also start to believe such things to be true. And best of all? It does not require any prerequisites to be true to be the case. In other words, such defenses are a flesh screen.

CHAPTER 6

Parental and Peer Influences

When it comes to teenage relationships, peers may not be the only people who matter. Research shows that family dynamics can have a significant impact on one's love life. Feelings and attitudes about dating can cast a shadow into one's adult relationships.

Children see and hear a lot, says Sarah Halpern-Meekin, a professor of human development and family studies at the University of Wisconsin-Madison. They learn from the stories of family members and the experiences of friends.

David Szwedo, a developmental psychologist, is a research assistant professor at Penn State. He does not care for the term "grounded" when parents restrict teens from going on dates; teenagers use technology and communicate in various ways. However, parents have the ability to shape their parents' attitudes and expectations about relationships.

Helicopter or snowplow parents can also indirectly influence their children's relationships. Halpern-Meekin is concerned. Of course, parents' driving intentions and kindness are important. However, we may become so absorbed in our children's lives that we become preoccupied with achievement and prevent our children from making their own decisions.

A nurturing parent can provide feedback and advice when teens feel drawn to a crush—something that Halpern-Meekin and her co-researchers asked many participants about. Many of them didn't talk to their parents because of the expressions of affection. However, numerous participants discussed romantic experiences growing up.

In terms of relationship values and concepts, friends and peers are influential. Some participants just used their peers as a point of reference for what an ideal partnership would look like and whether they liked someone. The other participants asked their friends and peers for advice on how to get closer to a crush. It's possible that their crush may lead them to day.

Impact of Family Dynamics on Teen Relationships

Most studies have found support for the link between perceived parental support and overall adolescent psychosocial function, including dating relationships. For example, adolescent perceptions of parental support have been linked to their positive dating relationship quality and positive association with friends and dating partners. One study found that adolescent reports of maternal positive behavioral control (adolescents' perceptions of parents' knowledge of their whereabouts) were significantly related to positive characteristics in dating partners. These findings underscore the importance of family dynamics.

Families provide an important context within which teens form their expectations of love and intimacy by providing models of couple relationships (parental modeling), by directly communicating to children about love and intimacy, and by connecting them with the world at large. Parental communication regarding love and dating has been found to operate in a "virtuous cycle": Research indicates that adolescents who talk with their parents about love and dating relationships are likely to have communication and relational skills associated with healthy dating relationships, basic self-esteem, and knowledge about love implicit in their everyday experiences. These qualities enable these dating-involved teens to establish trust in their parents and the quality of their advice about dating relationships that also translate to the quality of their family relationships; in turn, teens with positive family relationships continue to communicate with their parents about love and dating. Parental modeling of romantic love, including exhibiting emotional support and loving respect, contributes to children's understanding of a healthy love relationship by conveying positive lessons about marriage. Family systems theory helps us to understand that family dynamics (parental communication and parental modeling) influences directly, or indirectly through the adolescent's sense of family connectedness, many components of adolescent dating relationships.

CHAPTER 7

Digital Age Challenges

Challenges often arise in relationships when love transitions from platonic to something more. This gets exponentially more complex when the relationship exists primarily in a digital space. As social media and online dating disrupt the ways that we meet people and engage in romantic relationships, teens are trying to make sense of it all. But it's not just platforms like Instagram or Snapchat that have changed the game; communication in all forms has been revolutionized by technology. It can make relationships easier, but may also give way to added obstacles that call for new skills in negotiation.

Today's teens are digital natives, meaning they have largely grown up with access to digital technology like smartphones, tablets, and computers. This allows them to connect, communicate, and experiment sexually, even if they are not able to connect in person. Digital communication in the form of texting and messaging has also emerged as an integral part of teen friendships, as it empowers them to maintain constant contact and negotiate relational dynamics, or "tune relationships," with friends and partners throughout the day. This digital age brings with it a new set of both opportunities and risks that do not always mirror their offline counterpart. On the one hand, digital interfaces like texting and social media messages help teens by offering a buffer from in-person interactions and by providing nonverbal cues in the written form. On the other hand, questions such as sexting and the irrevocability of losing one's virginity with digital sex acts, calls for new skills of clear and careful communication.

Social Media and Teen Relationships

For many of today's adolescents, their initial romantic experiences are shaped by apps like TikTok and Instagram, where they simultaneously witness and participate in heartwarming meet-cutes, crushing rejections, and flirtatious debates in the comments section. Social media and video sharing platforms have become important cultural spaces where modern youth seek support and advice, gain access to previously hidden perspectives and resources, and share their attempts to pursue connections amidst a wide range of vulnerabilities and insecurities. Digital devices can also facilitate the continuation of relationships by offering teens the social courage to express their feelings through text message or the distance to take the blame for a breakup they feel unable to communicate in person. Users of these platforms become increasingly shaped by the affordances of the platform architecture itself with its default settings and invisible rules.

These platform affordances influence which of a user's social interactions with products, people, and content will be made visible to the other participants in the network and the ways in which they can present themselves and communicate with others. At the same time, users upload texts, images, and videos that draw on older, offline scripts of interpersonal communication and face-to-face romance, demonstrate a level of digital skill beyond that of many adults in their lives, and inflect these offline conventions with the material inequalities, injustices, and opportunities of the digital age. Platform affordances shape visibility, self-presentation, and content interaction, but in response, individual social media users shape the meanings and practices associated with the technical architecture. As a result, neither individual behavior nor the role of social media platforms can be fully understood in isolation.

CHAPTER 8

Cultural Perspectives on Teen Love

While many view teen relationships from a psychological and developmental perspective, it is also enlightening to consider how culture and, in a broader sense, "tradition" or "custom," shape young people's experience with love and romance. It is a cultural construct to categorize experiences as unique to young people. The ways in which young people engage in romantic relationships and process "crushes" are shaped by adults—family members, community members, teachers—both intentionally and inadvertently. Engaging with young people in diverse cultural contexts also reveals the myriad ways relationships—with family, friends, mates, and God—are important in their lives. Below are some ways we can understand teen romantic relationships through a cross-cultural lens.

- Activity: Some Inuit and Yup'ik cultures of Alaska discourage youth dating, encouraging them to become involved in activities that benefit the wider community. Some other youth speak fondly of friendships and relationships facilitated by shared activities and hobbies, describing a similar value. - Gendered Norms: Many Mayan families in Mexico and Guatemala do not encourage dating. Additionally, strict, chaperoned dating and long engagements before marriage are normal and expected in Muslim communities from Sudan to West Africa. - Power and Control: School-based abstinence clubs are common in the United States. These clubs perpetuate a social norm that girls should not be too interested in boys and teach boys to think of girls as unworthy of respect if they wear revealing clothing or are flirtatious. In Mayan Guatemala, it is normal for husbands to belittle and abuse their wives.

Cross-Cultural Views on Adolescent Romance

While the demographics of the teenagers we met at the beginning of this chapter varied considerably, our respondents were striking in their near-universal acknowledgment of romantic experiences among today's adolescents. Adolescence is a culturally constructed concept, as we stressed in the introduction to this book, and societies around the world have distinct social institutions and values associated with the years between biological maturation and transitions—educational, sexual, and vocational—to adulthood. Adolescence itself may be shorter or longer in some societies than others, and more or less constrained by specific responsibilities and rules. In this section, we will explore the cross-cultural perspectives our respondents have presented. To what extent are young people, even in scientifically and technologically advanced societies, shielded from many adult privileges and responsibilities, yet also from the possibilities for finding romance and sexual pleasure?

The subsections below examine cross-cultural perspectives on adolescent romance, based on the information provided by teen ethnographers in this chapter. In discussing the many cultural differences that emerge, teen researchers have shared the social norms as well as the experiences of young people in India, Indonesia, Mexico, Nigeria, Slovakia, and Ukraine. Data, mostly collected a decade ago, show a range of responses to the question "Are romantic relationships common for people your age in your society?" Responses to this question are drawn from research involving young people from the places listed above. Some teenagers' responses elaborated upon the nature of these relationships in their societies, referencing considerations of social class, geographic origin within their country, and differing regional values.

CHAPTER 9

Gender and Sexuality in Teen Relationships

Teen love is filled with diversity. Some teens are gay, some are straight, some are bisexual or pansexual, and some might be questioning or uncertain about their romantic urges. Some might not even be interested in relationships at all. And many people's sense of gender doesn't match the male/female two-choice system our society has given them. What's crucial about gender and sexuality is that they mean more than physical attraction. Gender and sexuality are much more about who you are than about who you love. Still, some teens find that they need specialized advice about being in a relationship as a member of the LGBTQ+ community—it can be challenging in ways that relationships of heterosexual teens are not.

It is important to keep in mind that some gender and sexual identities might be more accepted in some cultures or across some geographic spaces than in others. For example, some areas of the US may be more accepting of gender nonconforming and transgender teens than others. However, it is important for everyone in the audience to understand diverse romantic experiences. Teens are capable of many kinds of loving experiences, even if they don't consider these to be romantic experiences. Words and phrases like "stepping out" of your comfort zone or being "able" to engage in a particular kind of romantic intimacy may appear inadvertently prescriptive or shaming. It is important to include everyone, regardless of their preferences.

Exploring LGBTQ+ Teen Love

Ambiguity and confusion surrounding the rules of dating and love are significant among queer youths who navigate the rules of straight love and their own queerness while trying to create homosexual love. Complications of parents who are inconsistent in their attempts to protect versus further injure their experiential transition have been a common thread in the lives of same-sex adolescent daters. On one hand, these new friends are portrayed as the same-sex love partner who is "just like everybody else" and desires to make mom understand that. On the other hand, same-sex friendships that are more intense are dismissed as normal small-group behavior and should not conflict with female friendships where the feeling of disappointed young love is not discussed. For "real life," where she dates boys, she seems to be so desperate to deny that the possibility of dating is completely dismissed. She isn't gay, even significantly more anonymous on social networking sites. This hide-n-seek game of romantic friendship would be a good starting point for my final chapter on gay and lesbian experiences and healing after coming out; it seems to be sadder. It might have been just a transition delay. I will use them if I am not personable elsewhere.

However, the life of gay, lesbian, and bisexual teenager-daters is not as hard as it was in the previous decade, although the bond of society is still fraught and sometimes divides rather than unites. During the last twenty years, the presence of support programs and teaching resources has increased amidst the hetero-normative trauma inflicted on younger students. I reaffirm the importance of a cultural competency framework, organizational, and reading list on the website as a gesture of practical power reinforcement strategies. Conditions that restrict teen acceptance of his or her sexual orientation or that condemn the individuals who show a sexual minority status tend to reinforce the internal institutions and social delivery system. In turn, the fall in self-esteem can lead to rejection, guilt, and self-condemnation, including the belief that one is sick. Regardless of the tenuous position the university's conservative mission takes in providing editorial space for Dr. Vincent Beatty of the Psychology Analysis Department, it's important to remember two things that discredit his article. Adpulmo Counseling Services is dedicated to the physical and mental safety of the university community while treating this article in time. In addition, according to the position of the American Psychological Association, sexual orientation cannot be changed. Hundreds of people decide to bring healing and acceptance to their own gifts within sexual orientation. Pride Alliance supports everyone working on the self-press release, including adults experiencing SSA. Family, friends, and gay, lesbian, bisexual, and others may honor, validate, and help them in finding a growing relationship with. Therefore, labels move and grow because depth and duration of persistence are better teachers than culture if a lifelong partner provides the true way of life, potential, and internal freedom.

CHAPTER 10

Mental Health and Teen Love

The statistics consistently bear out anxiety's dominance in these young people. For those capable of putting into words their struggle to emerge from that constant state of dread, common enough for their peers, the beginning of a romantic relationship can actually mean the beginning of facing some of that anxiety—albeit anxiety unique to and largely symptomatic of a particular relationship. Love requires trust—trust that the other person knows my flaws and loves me anyway, trust that the other person is honest about his or her feelings, trust that the outcome of this dating relationship can be a productive, if sometimes painful, decision-making process rather than a referendum on my worth as a human being.

Though the role of the family is irreplaceable in fostering self-worth, church can also serve as a corrective. When teens don't receive certain validation at home, many begin to look for it in their romantic partners. Consequently, we should not only celebrate teen love, acknowledging it as an important part of their emotional lives, we should also be watching for signs of damage that could occur if that perfect emotion isn't received: unchanged high expectations, impatience, depression or anxiety, and even suicidal thoughts when dating doesn't measure up. We can and will help all people experience that joy, but we might save our teens from this additional anguish which love relationships can harbor, simply by looking for the second-level presumed mental health vulnerabilities present underneath their high smiles.

Anxiety and Depression in Teen Relationships

Teen's love could make you think back to sweet memories from your past or dread screaming and slammed doors. As noted by an online publisher and their contributors who recently spent a week looking at all things 15, we also understand that speaking about teenage's first loves may be a sensitive subject. For teenagers, falling in love is not as simple and pleasant as those commonplace words make it out to be. Love begins to be tangled with feelings of self-doubt. It is simple to see why there is a strong link between love and teenage anxiety and depression, particularly for girls. While love may be toxic, it is essential to be aware of your standards and to care for people that you date or care about deeply if they get into a high school relationship.

High school romance certainly has its difficulties, even if it's heartwarming. According to the CDC, there are close to 8 percent more students who report being in relationships in large cities than in rural areas. Fights and separations bring drama and conflict into larger school systems. Not disclosing your commitment or dating status can still be an invitation to tease, suspicion, and distinction. Depression is hidden a lot more and may be sparked by a secluded romantic failing or the lack thereof. The reality is that teenagers feel unhappy when they are in their relationship and do not see the top. Teenagers are not aware of so many young teenagers among them. Sympathy is the only pediatric intervention.

CHAPTER 11

Educational Interventions for Healthy Teen Relatio

Over the past 15 years, the federal government has supported various demonstration and research projects aimed at helping young people acquire critical components necessary for a healthy relationship. But, as is true for sex education, most youth do not and will not take advantage of relationship education classes provided in a clinical setting. The United States has undoubtedly considered integrating some version of sex education into the nation's schools, and state requirements for its inclusion have been broadening since the 1970s following precedent-setting legal decisions suggesting that sex education is a respectable endeavor for public schools. To promote healthy teen relationships, building upon the ample, multi-year precedent of working with schools as venues for providing relationship education to the general student body (rather than only to those couples having demonstrated destructive conflict), is the recommendable approach.

Comprehensive educational interventions aim to cover essential areas having identifiable links to a safe and fulfilling relationship like: communication and interpersonal skills, values and expectations regarding intimate relationships, cohabitation and marriage, individual growth and development, relationship abuse and violence, skills for time and money management and general problem solving, life courses of peers in success and challenge, what helps marriages and other romantic unions go well, as well as job-related, financial, and computer skills. Educating the school-aged also enables those who have yet to form their first dating relationship to distinguish between a positive two-person transpersonal commitment and casual dating. It can contribute to the diminution of juvenile delinquency by modeling and practicing good institutional behavior. Also, providing ways to prevent problems makes inherent value sense for a society which believes its citizens are entitled to protection.

Incorporating Relationship Education in Schools
Practical ideas for incorporating relationship education in schools School-based relationship education offers a promising mechanism for reaching most young people with evidence-based knowledge and skills, and curricula should consider the provision needs of early prevention. Curriculum buffers also exist to help stressed teachers manage stress associated with new social, emotional, and academic life. Teaching positive teen relationships has the potential to improve relationships. School and adolescent community-based programs reduce and treat violence, sexual and dating violence, and promote sexual health, but few have teen social relationships or pending approval. That could lead to serious violence, including mass shootings. Education by the school can provide an equitable framework for starting all young people, making it the oldest victim capable of helping adults in the community to help move always higher, eventually preventing intimate partner violence.

The school is the main place where people graduate to become adults and the main source of support for all children in the United States. In the United Youth Bullying Awareness Month. Ask your teacher and staff how to integrate information and techniques for developing relationships and creating a culture of allies every day of the year! Our 7-day interdisciplinary week curriculum designed for middle and high school with PHSB national recommendation posters will be hosted on October/November 2020. Call our office at 202-800-8990 or email referrals@loveandbind.us!

CHAPTER 12

Research and Statistics on Teen Love

Research by the non-profit organization, Child Trends, and the UK-based charity, Relate, collected data from parents, teenagers, and teachers and experts in child development to learn more about teenage love. Here are some facts and statistics.

All interviews with experts showed that the "teen years are characterized by an interest in romantic and sexual relationships." The researchers interviewed over 600 parents of teenagers between the ages of 13 and 18 about their child's experience of love. While some parents reported that their children did not form any romantic attachments or demonstrate an interest in love relationships, over half of the parents reported that their teenagers reported having a "love interest." Comments from the parents indicated that there may have been some differences in intensity and interest from male to female and from 13-year-olds to 18-year-olds, but the data do not reflect age or gender differences. A 2007 survey by the National Campaign to Prevent Teen Pregnancy in the USA asked 1,000 random teenagers between the ages of 12 and 19 about love. Just under half, or 48%, said that they were in a current love relationship, while 25% said that they had a past love relationship. Children at the ages of 12-15 and

16-19 were equally likely to report a love relationship during the past year. Non-Hispanic White teenagers were more likely to have had a love relationship than non-White teens. Irish 12-13-year-olds were more likely to have had past love relationships than African-Americans. Only 36% of African-American teenagers had reported a relationship within the past year. In each age group, a higher percentage of males reported being in a love relationship than females.

Trends in Teen Dating Behavior

In this section, we will investigate specific trends and behavioral patterns for teen dating. We will address questions such as whether teens are dating at all, the frequency of dating behavior, and whether these trends are transitory, somewhat down pre-COVID conditions, or structural, meaning data are reflecting a true change in teen dating culture and social script. Additionally, we seek to identify whether exclusionary factors (problems in their schools, communities, families) help clarify shifts in dating behavior. As mentioned, data on behavior indicate that less physical dating occurs in the present than has for some years, but the psychological nature of romantic involvements is now deeper than it was at its nadir in the early digital landscape of 2010.

Cherlin et al. used OSG data from 2005, 2001, and 1997 to look at some dating behaviors of teenagers aged 15–18. The questionnaire employed did not ask whether individuals had been on a date, but whether they had been on a 'real date' with someone they do not go with in the previous three months. In 1997, 56% of teenagers reported going on a 'real date', and this had declined to 40% by 2005, with virtually no change across subsequent generations. Mulford and Giordano complement this finding, as in their qualitative research of rural adolescents, the authors found a portion of participants lamenting the decline of boys inviting them to go to the movies. Participants opined that parents' new micro-management dating plan of providing rides and chaperoning events contributed to less romantic privacy and opportunities to hook up. Thus, marriageable status, driven in part by gender relations and parental socialization patterns, set the context for romantic involvement.

CHAPTER 13

Conclusion and Future Directions

Arguably, any or all of these topics could serve as the basis for a meaningful conversation in group therapy with young clients. But we suggest focusing primarily on repairing the identity structures of young people who feel psychologically unworthy, especially if they have a history of bullying. When we fail to address shame at its root, we find that not only does psychodynamic psychotherapy all too easily devolve into mere coping strategies, but that such therapy can actually cause further psychological harm. Shame can confirm feelings of irredeemable worthlessness, exacerbate and even radicalize feelings of anti-social revenge fantasy, lead to addictive behavior, or reinforce behaviors beholden to toxic social norms that do not help young people heal and grow.

The stigma and marginalization that the individually bullied child experiences may need a group context to correct, but this is unlikely to be achieved by a support group that works to excuse the bully. While no one should be limited to their worst deed, doing the work to interrupt systemic patterns of behavior involves taking accountability for the specific destruction one has caused. Furthermore, worthy of note is the disproportionately high rates of depression and suicide attempts in bulimic adolescents.

This essay has worked to avoid recommending any one way to be a teenager in love. There may, however, be less to fear in allowing the more emotionally intelligent adults to share a little of their hard-earned wisdom without having to constantly phrase their wisdom in teenage language, especially if an ideology in societal habit persists that forces young people to grow up and solve problems they should not be solving yet. It is clear that pursuing these directions would suggest that adolescents' transition into becoming the sort of adult in a meaningful and thriving romantic relationship would become more likely. Regardless of if adolescence is eventually worded in the language of tragic romantic love or not, we cannot neglect important means and possibilities of romantic agency and change; without these, the very essence of romance's charm and attraction is lost.

Emerging Trends in Teen Love Research

In this monograph, we focus on two areas that are evolving in the research on teen love. First, we highlight emerging trends, some forming the basis of this publication and some providing another avenue for future inquiry in the field of romantic relationships. Second, we present a collection of empirical or literature review findings about adolescence and teen romantic relationships in a series of 13 chapters, plus this introductory chapter. In the remainder of this introduction, we discuss some of these "in-process" emerging trends and a few additional areas we find may be ripe for continued exploration.

The research tracks and travels with the shifting and morphing landscape of adolescent relationships - that strikes the authors as one promising area to delve more deeply into. Charting a "snapshot" of teen love that "looks" different than what has been studied in previous decades, specifically highlighting the many and varied ways that adolescence is and is not changing. The chapters in these sections have reminded us of several assumptions from a prior time that have gone unchallenged, providing a host of intriguing questions about new developmental and cultural trends. This interest is focused in a larger sense on the cultural microcosm of adolescence and its links to the larger world, but does so by way of understanding teen love. Moreover, we find that our chapters present in-process conversations around power, equity versus equality, and the need for innovative analyses related to these topics. In all, we believe that these trends provide some reflective conclusions that "look forward" while also working within the present and past in different and compelling ways.